A Pillar Box Red Publication

we ♥ you...
LMFAO
A 2013 ANNUAL

Written by Sarah Milne
Designed by Nicky Regan

CONTENTS

THE STORY SO FAR

It may seem like LMFAO, or at least their amazing tunes, have been around for years – probably because they are so catchy and once you hear them you never forget them! But, as a band LMFAO have only officially been around since 2006, and their first hit, 'I'm In Miami', only started bubbling up from the underground dance scene in 2008.

But, the boys have known each other much longer than that. Indeed, Stefan Kendal Gordy and Skyler Austen Gordy, or Redfoo and SkyBlu, as they are better known, are in fact related, with Redfoo being SkyBlu's uncle (there's only an eleven year age gap between the two). So, no interviewer ever has to ask them 'where did you meet?' – they've always been part of each other's lives.

Growing up in Pacific Palisades, an up market neighbourhood of Los Angeles, the boys were always surrounded by good music. Redfoo's father (SkyBlu's grandfather) is Berry Gordy, a legendary figure in the US, and indeed the world's music scene. As the founder of Motown records, he has made music for some of the most amazing names of the 20th century including Diana Ross, Smokey Robinson, Stevie Wonder and The Jacksons.

After a childhood of hanging around with each other and being exposed to such amazing music, the boys formed a duo in 2006, originally calling themselves 'Sexe Dudes' (we think they were being a bit tongue in cheek). They stuck with this name until they mentioned it to Redfoo's grandmother, who suggested politely that it might not be the best name for them. Indeed, she signed her message "lmfao" and the boys took that abbreviation and made it their own – 'loving my friends and others', though some people think it stands for something quite different...

After playing various clubs and DJ sets (both the boys still DJ regularly), LMFAO signed to Interscope Records in 2008 and released the Party Rock EP in July of that year, which included LMFAO's first single, 'I'm In Miami', released December 2008. The single did fairly well, but it was really in 2009 when it became the smash hit, when it was used as a theme tune for the US reality show, 'Kourtney and Khloe Take Miami'.

In 2010, LMFAO recorded their second album, and this included the singles 'Party Rock Anthem', 'Champagne Showers' and 'I'm Sexy and I Know It' with its memorable video. These amazing tunes propelled the boys onto the world's stage, and in 2012, they even performed with Madonna as part of the halftime entertainment at the Super Bowl, watched by an estimated 111 million people worldwide.

With a heavy tour schedule in summer 2012, and more planned for 2013, we'll hopefully get to see more of the LMFAO boys in person and hear a few new singles too. We're never sorry for Party Rocking!

we love you... LMFAO

BAND NAME: LMFAO.

BAND MEMBERS: Redfoo & SkyBlu.

BAND FORMED: 2006, Los Angeles.

ORIGINS OF NAME: The boys claim it stands for 'Loving My Friends and Others'.

ALBUMS: Party Rock, 2009; Sorry For Party Rocking, 2011.

SINGLES: 8 of their own, 22 with other artists, either as featured artists or pure collaborations.

AWARDS: 11 so far, many more to come!

BEST KNOWN FOR: Party Rock Anthem, Sexy & I Know It, I'm in Miami.

MUSIC STYLE: Party Rock.

DRESS STYLE: Neon, shiny, crazy party gear.

PERFORMING STYLE: Only one way to describe it - *pure energy*!

FACT FILE

Redfoo was born Stefan Kendal Gordy on September 3, 1975 in Los Angeles. His mother Nancy Leiviska, worked at the Motown Record label, which his father, the legendary Berry Gordy, founded in 1960.

SkyBlu was born Skyler Austen Gordy on August 23, 1986. His father is Redfoo's half brother, making him Redfoo's nephew, and Berry Gordy's grandson.

Growing up in such a musical family was bound to have an effect on the two boys, as indeed it has done on the whole Gordy family. Berry Gordy has been in the music business since the 1950s, when he started out by opening a record shop that featured mostly jazz songs. Through some connections, Berry then started writing songs with his sister Gwen for stars such as Jackie Wilson and Etta James.

A FAMILY AFFAIR

It's a well-known fact that Redfoo and SkyBlu are related, but just how, and what were both their childhoods like?

Berry started his first record label in 1959, but it was in 1960 when Motown was born that the label produced hit after hit for many of the most famous stars of the day, from Smokey Robinson to Stevie Wonder, Marvin Gaye to The Jackson 5.

Both the boys grew up listening to these legendary artists and indeed meeting more than a few of them over the years. The Motown label was really considered to be one big family, and it was not unusual for the family to have artists round to the house.

Family get togethers were often musical affairs, with stages and performances, and both the boys have said that they would try to 'outdo' one another at them.

Redfoo claims that whenever SkyBlu managed to put on a better performance, he would go jump behind the drum kit and thrash out a few solos to keep the folks happy.

Growing up in a family so pivotal to the American music scene has meant the boys are both excited by, and knowledgeable of, the record business. Redfoo has stated that his father is very proud of their achievements, and so he should be.

WORDSEARCH

Can you find the following LMFAO related words hidden in the wordsearch below?

If you get stuck you can find the answers at the back on page 60!

Rocking
Redfoo
SkyBlu
Gordy
Palisades
Guetta
Kesha
Sexy
Shufflebot
Madonna
Party
GoonRock

Y	K	A	H	S	E	K	G	M	T	Y	T
L	Q	L	K	C	O	R	N	O	O	G	O
T	K	B	P	C	N	X	I	M	W	P	B
P	A	R	T	Y	K	N	K	R	B	A	E
Y	S	K	Y	B	L	U	C	F	M	L	L
B	X	Y	W	Y	G	A	O	P	Z	I	F
F	N	E	N	W	N	O	R	G	C	S	F
D	X	Y	S	N	O	G	U	T	Z	A	U
H	L	F	O	F	B	E	O	X	J	D	H
Y	D	D	D	Y	T	J	V	R	L	E	S
W	A	E	P	T	V	C	J	L	D	S	V
M	R	R	A	J	Z	M	D	X	L	Y	R

LMFAO may not have been around for many years, but what they lack in experience; they make up for in pure energy. Their hits are fast, funky and all about having fun. Infact, your party playlist can take a back seat – just put one of their albums on repeat and get shufflin'!

DISCOGRAPHY

ALBUMS

2009
Party Rock Went Gold in Australia.

2011
Sorry For Party Rocking Went four times Platinum in Australia, two times Platinum in Canada and Gold in US, Ireland and New Zealand.

SINGLES

2008
I'm In Miami

2009
La la la

Shots (featuring Lil Jon)

Yes

2011
Party Rock Anthem (featuring Lauren Bennett and Goon Rock) Went to number one in nine countries.

Champagne Showers (Featuring Natalia Kills).

Sexy and I Know It Went to number one in four countries and top ten in another six.

2012
Sorry for Party Rocking Went to number one in four countries and top ten in another six.

SINGLES AS FEATURED ARTISTS

2008
Shooting Star (David Rush, featuring Kevin Rudolf, LMFAO and Pitbull).

2010
Outta Your Mind (Lil Jon featuring LMFAO).

Gettin' Over You (David Guetta featuring Chris Willis, Fergie and LMFAO).

2012
Livin' My Love (Steve Aoki featuring LMFAO and Nervo).

Drink (Lil Jon featuring LMFAO).

we love you... LMFAO

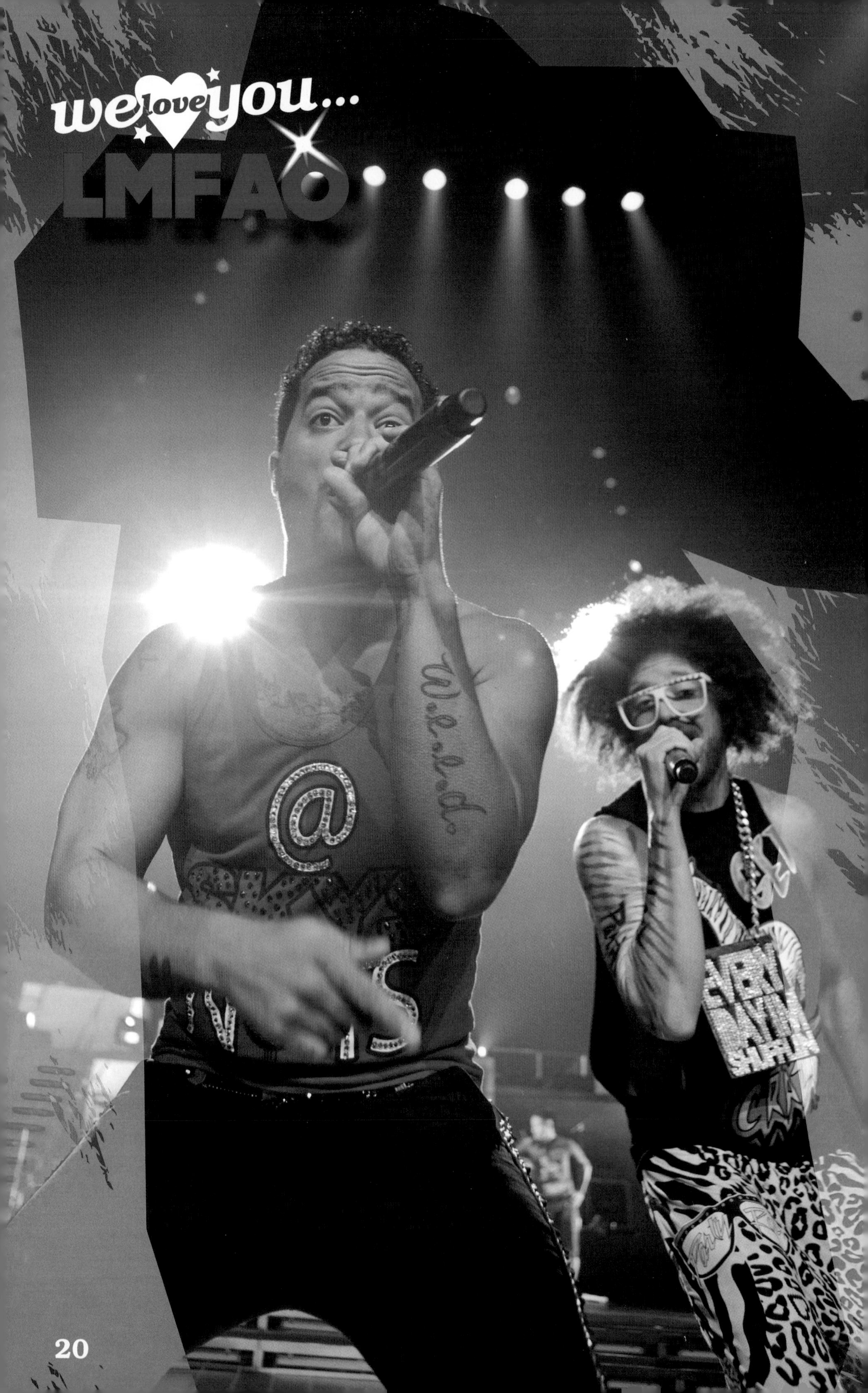

CROSSWORD

The answers are at the back on page 60!

ACROSS

1 Which Florida party spot are LMFAO in? (5)

6 The boys sang about Champagne .... – better take your umbrella (7)

8 Will.i.am is LMFAO's friend and Executive Producer. What is the name of his band? (13)

9 Dance craze, LMFAO style (3, 7)

11 LMFAO second album, Sorry for .... (5, 7)

12 Redfoo's 'real' name is .... Gordy (6)

DOWN

2 The Queen of Pop performed with the boys at the 2012 Super Bowl (7)

3 Famous relative could be a tasty treat .... Gordy (5)

4 Location for the 'I'm Sexy' video, or an Italian city .... Beach (6)

5 SkyBlu is known to his family as .... (6)

7 Dance troupe often seen performing with the boys, could be an adventurous lot (5, 4)

10 The boys are related – Redfoo is SkyBlu's .... (5)

we *love* you...
LMFAO

If you've ever seen Redfoo and SkyBlu live, or even just watched LMFAO videos, you'll know how infectious and energetic their performances are. Add this to some amazingly catchy tunes, and it's no wonder that their videos have triggered a wave of copycats from all over the world, from famous folk to the general public. Here's our pick of the best.

POKEMON PARTY ROCK

It may not have the highest production values, but this parody will appeal to the geeks and gamers out there. Best moment – getting so many Pokemon character names in there!

FAMOUS LMFAO PARODIES!

TOM DALEY AND THE TEAM GB DIVE SQUAD

Taking some time off from their strict training schedule (!), the boys from the UK diving team made this video. They may just be lip synching to the original, but they've got the beach bodies to show off! Best moment – the slightly embarrassing dancing!

EVERY DAY I'M DUMBLEDORE!

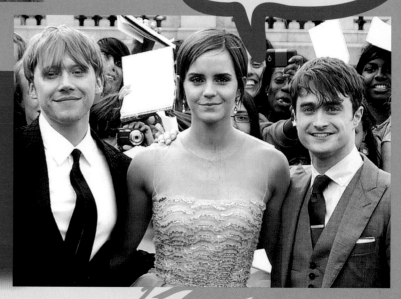

POTTER ROCK ANTHEM

The Harry Potter themed copycat video is very high quality, with good singing and acting, fun costumes and even the lyrics have been altered well. Best moment – 'Every Day I'm Dumbledore'.

GOTTA FEED EVERYBODY!

I'M GASSY AND I'M BLOATED

This parody takes the subject of excess wind and applies it to LMFAO's biggest hit. Funny, and well produced. Best moment – 'Bubbles in my tummy'.

I'M FARMING AND I GROW IT

Three farming brothers with their agricultural take on the hit. Best moment – 'Gotta Feed Everybody'.

I MAKE ART

I'M ELMO AND I KNOW IT

You couldn't fail to love this age-appropriate version, featuring little red Sesame Street cutie, Elmo. Best moment – 'Kids look at these crayons… I make art'.

BRIGHT COLOURS

The boys are never far away from the brightest of colours, from neon pink, to acid yellow. While they like to mix and match their colours, you can pull it off by teaming brights with something a bit darker.

GLASSES

Usually thick rimmed, one white pair and one black pair. Do they really need them for seeing properly? DO we really care? Fashion glasses rock.

BIG TRAINERS

Essential for shuffling!

GET THE PARTY ROCKIN' LOOK

As well as great tunes, one of LMFAO's signatures is their amazing, sometimes crazy, sense of style. They even have their own line of clothing called, what else? – Party Rock Clothing. And, while it might not be a look you could get away with completely on the streets, by just taking a few of the LMFAO style essentials, you'll still be able to get the Party Rocking look...

ANIMAL PRINTS

Tiger, leopard, zebra – the boys don't really care which wild animal they look like, as long as they've got some on their body at all times. And if it clashes, then even better!

BIG HAIR

Essential for bouncing around on the dance floor. Backcomb and hairspray your way to LMFAO locks.

GOLD CHAINS

Channeling B.A. Baracus from The A-Team, LMFAO like to pile on the gold chains, the thicker the better.

LEATHER JACKETS

A bit of rocker action here – the boys are often to be seen in a leather (or pleather) jacket – makes a change from all those clashing colours!

LYCRA

Essential for showing off that body and allowing for maximum freedom of movement on the dance floor.

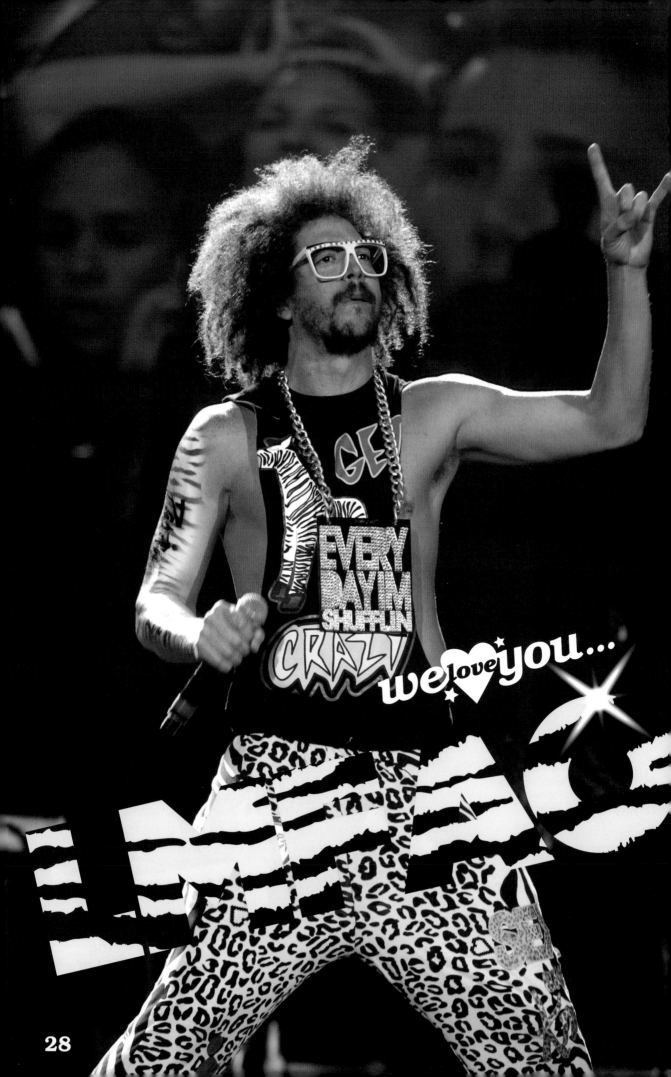

we love you...

we love you... LMFAO

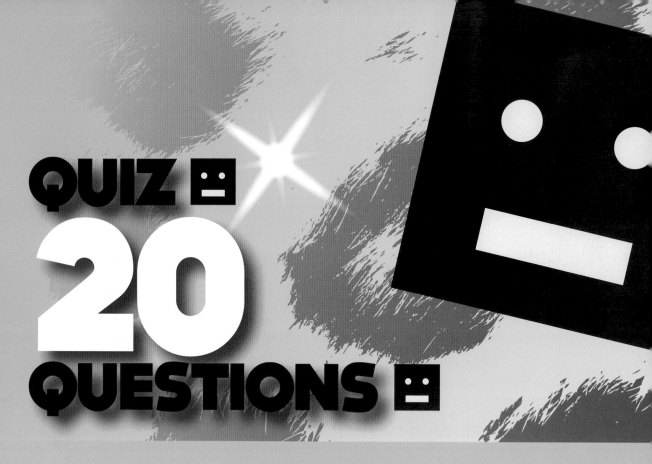

QUIZ
20
QUESTIONS

The answers are at the back on page 61!

1 Which legendary record producer is Redfoo's father AND SkyBlu's grandfather?

2 Which well off neighbourhood of Los Angeles did the boys grow up in?

3 Which famous singer and producer has been a friend with Redfoo since they were children?

4 What year did LMFAO officially form?

5 What does LMFAO stand for?

6 And what did the boys originally call themselves?

7 Which megastar did LMFAO perform with as part of the 2012 Super Bowl half-time entertainment?

8 And how many people are estimated to have watched the performance?

9 Can you name LMFAO's albums?

10 What has been LMFAO's biggest hit single to date?

11   Which US female singer did LMFAO open for during her 2011 tour?

12   Which US reality TV show used 'I'm In Miami' for the title song?

13   Which dance move do the boys like to get into each of their performances?

14   What's the name of the LMFAO clothing range?

15   What's the name of the robot headed dancer that often appears in LMFAO videos/performances?

16   Which famous LA landmark was the location for the 'I'm Sexy and I Know It' video shoot?

17   Which British sporting team, headed by Tom Daley, has created an 'I'm Sexy and I Know It' parody video?

18   What genre of music is LMFAO credited with inventing?

19   Which English singer/songwriter featured in the hit 'Champagne Showers'?

20   How do LMFAO explain their attitude to life?

we love you...
LMFAO

32

Though LMFAO have officially been together since 2006, it's only in the past few years that they've really broken through to the mainstream, and since they have, the awards have been flowing (quite right too). Here's a run-down of the main gongs they've won or been nominated for so far...

2010

Party Rock, nominated for Best Dance/Electronica Album at The Grammys.

2011

Party Rock Anthem nominated for Choice Summer Song at the Teen Choice Awards.

Party Rock Anthem nominated for Best Choreography at the MTV Music Video Awards.

LMFAO nominated for Favourite Pop/Rock Band/Duo/Group at the American Music Awards.

LMFAO nominated for Best New Band and Best Push at the MTV Europe Music Awards.

2012

Party Rock Anthem nominated for Song of the Year at The People's Choice Awards.

Party Rock Anthem nominated for Music Video of the Year at The People's Choice Awards.

Party Rock Anthem wins Music Video of the Year at the NRJ Music Awards.

Party Rock Anthem wins Favourite Song of the Year at the Kids' Choice Awards.

Party Rock Anthem wins five awards at the Billboard Music awards and is nominated for another two.

Party Rock Anthem wins Best Music at the MTV Movie Awards.

Sexy and I Know It nominated for four awards at the Billboard Music Awards.

Sexy and I Know It wins International Video of the Year at the MuchMusic awards.

Sorry For Party Rocking nominated for International Album of the Year at the Juno Awards.

LMFAO win International Group/Duo of the Year at the NRJ Music Awards.

LMFAO nominated for Favourite Music Group at the Kids' Choice Awards.

LMFAO win Best Group/Duo at the Billboard Music awards.

AWARDS

33

ON TOUR

No matter how many times you listen to LMFAO in your own home, simply nothing compares to seeing them perform live. From the killer tunes and high energy dance routines to the louder than loud costumes and amazing light shows,

LMFAO on tour is a must for any real fan, and on stage is really where they come into their own. Even seeing a recording of one of their live performances gives an exciting glimpse into what it would be like to see the real thing. Getting up on stage and rocking a crowd is something the boys love doing as separate artists and together as LMFAO, and here's what they've done already, as well as what's planned for the future...

2010

LMFAO accompany The Black Eyed Peas on tour for their 'The E.N.D. World Tour 2010' all over North America.

2011

LMFAO are the opening act for Ke$ha's 'Get Sleazy Tour'.

LMFAO go on their first tour of Asia, going to Singapore, the Philippines, Taiwan and Malaysia.

2012

The boys perform with Madonna as part of the half-time entertainment at the 2012 Super Bowl. The performance is seen by an estimated 111 million people worldwide.

LMFAO embark on a summer tour of Europe, playing at many UK festivals, such as V Festival and Hyde Park.

2013 and beyond...

LMFAO will continue to rock the party all over the world and could be coming to a venue near you...

FAMOUS FANS & COLLABO-RATORS

LMFAO are a band that love to work with other artists and this in turn means that other artists love to work with them. And of course, their high-energy enthusiasm means the boys get asked to perform at lots of celebrity parties, where they make many celebrity fans...

WILL.I.AM

Childhood friend of Redfoo since they were in 7th grade, Will and the boys have always been interested in, and contributed to each other's work.

NATALIA KILLS

English singer/songwriter and actress, Natalia performed with the boys on 'Champagne Showers', and is signed to the same label as the band.

LIL JON

Lil Jon and LMFAO have worked on a number of tracks together, including their hit 'Shots' and his 'Outta Your Mind' and 'Drunk'.

JUSTIN BIEBER

JB is known to enjoy the Party Rock, and recently tweeted that "I'm Sexy and I Know It". Whether he was referring to the LMFAO hit or just his own reflection, we just can't say.

LAUREN BENNETT

British singer, dancer and model, Lauren is the new lead singer of the Pussycat Dolls, and featured on 'Party Rock Anthem'.

MADONNA

LMFAO worked with the Queen of Pop on tracks from her latest album MDNA, 'Give Me All Your Lovin'. They also performed with her as part of the half time entertainment at the Super Bowl 2012.

THE QUEST CREW

LA based street dance crew were winners of the third series of hit US show, 'America's Best Dance Crew'. Members of the crew have performed with LMFAO during their performances on 'So You Think You Can Dance' and on live sets. Crew member Hokuto Konishi choreographed the videos for 'Party Rock Anthem' and 'I'm Sexy and I Know It', as well as appearing in the video for 'Champagne Showers'.

GOONROCK

American producer, songwriter and musician, co-wrote and co-produced tracks on 'Sorry For Party Rocking' including hits 'Party Rock Anthem' and 'I'm Sexy and I Know It'.

we love you... LMFAO

39

FRED ASTAIRE

The world-famous dancing film star of the 1920s and 1930s has been quoted as a dancer that the boys like to watch for inspiration.

INFLUENCES

Coming from a legendary family in the US record business, the boys were both surrounded by a lot of different musical influences form an early age, and that's definitely reflected in their Party Rock style today. Redfoo really loved rappers and R&B, while both the boys loved classic rock bands too. Today, their mix of high-energy dance music with a hint of rock has proved a winning combination!

LED ZEPPELIN

70's rockers Led Zeppelin may seem like an unusual influence for LMFAO, but maybe it was the big hair and tight jeans of lead singer Robert Plant that helped the boys perfect their look.

MICHAEL JACKSON

The Jackson family, and especially Michael worked closely with Berry Gordy (Redfoo's father/SkyBlu's grandfather) throughout his career, so it's no surprise that the boys love his work.

THE BEATLES

One of the first British bands to make it big in America, the boys love The Beatles' ability to write catchy tunes.

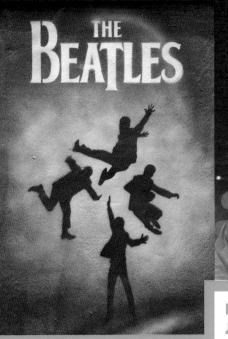

THE BLACK EYED PEAS

Redfoo and will.i.am have known each other since the 7th grade, and so the two have always been closely involved in each others' work – Will is now their Executive Producer. You'll often find a Black Eyed Peas number slipping into an LMFAO DJ set.

JAMES BROWN

The legendary American singer, songwriter and musician is credited as being the Godfather of Soul, and the Inventor of Funk. He started performing in the 1950s and continued right up till his death in 2006. His influence can be seen in many types of music around today.

EDDIE MURPHY/ JIM CARREY

SkyBlu has stated that these two comedians influence his performances, and he liked to imitate them when he was younger.

we love you...
LMFAO

NAME THAT TUNE!

The answers are at the back on page 61!

1 I got that devilish flow rock and roll no halo

We party rock yea! that's the crew that I'm repping

On a rise to the top no Led in our Zeppelin

2 Hey, you're looking kind of cute in that polka dot bikini, girl

3 This is how I roll, animal print, pants outta control,

It's Redfoo with the big afro

And like Bruce Leroy I got the glow

4 I walk in the club with a bottle or two

shake it, spray it on a body or two

And walk out the party with a hottie or two

5 Yoyo, everybody's on the floor

I can see your hands up

From the stage to the door

Calvin Harris on the deck

LMFAO's on the checks

6 What happens at the party stays at the party

What happens at the club stays at the club

44

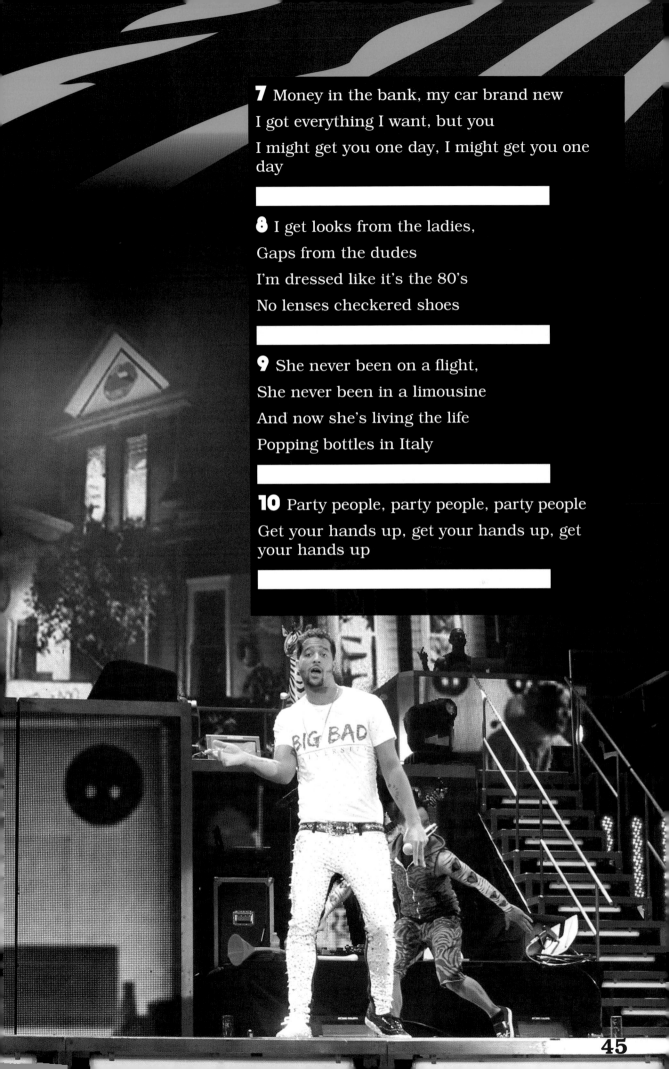

7 Money in the bank, my car brand new
I got everything I want, but you
I might get you one day, I might get you one day

8 I get looks from the ladies,
Gaps from the dudes
I'm dressed like it's the 80's
No lenses checkered shoes

9 She never been on a flight,
She never been in a limousine
And now she's living the life
Popping bottles in Italy

10 Party people, party people, party people
Get your hands up, get your hands up, get your hands up

we love you...
LMFAO

There's only 11 years difference in age, but Redfoo is SkyBlu's uncle.

SkyBlu always wears odd shoes.

Berry Gordy – legendary founder of Motown Records, is Redfoo's father and SkyBlu's Grandfather.

Redfoo never has lenses in his frames.

When they were younger, the boys would try to outperform each other at family occasions to see who worked the crowd better.

Redfoo is a former brother-in law of Jermaine Jackson, Michael's older brother.

Redfoo started to grow his afro in 2005.

They love the work and look of US comedian Eddie Murphy during the 1980s/1990s.

SkyBlu claims that he was attacked by US politician Mitt Romney in 2010. Following the incident, SkyBlu was escorted off the aeroplane by the authorities.

SkyBlu has a tattoo in tribute to Michael Jackson on his arm, taken from the Moonwalker video.

Redfoo plays the drums.

TRIVIA

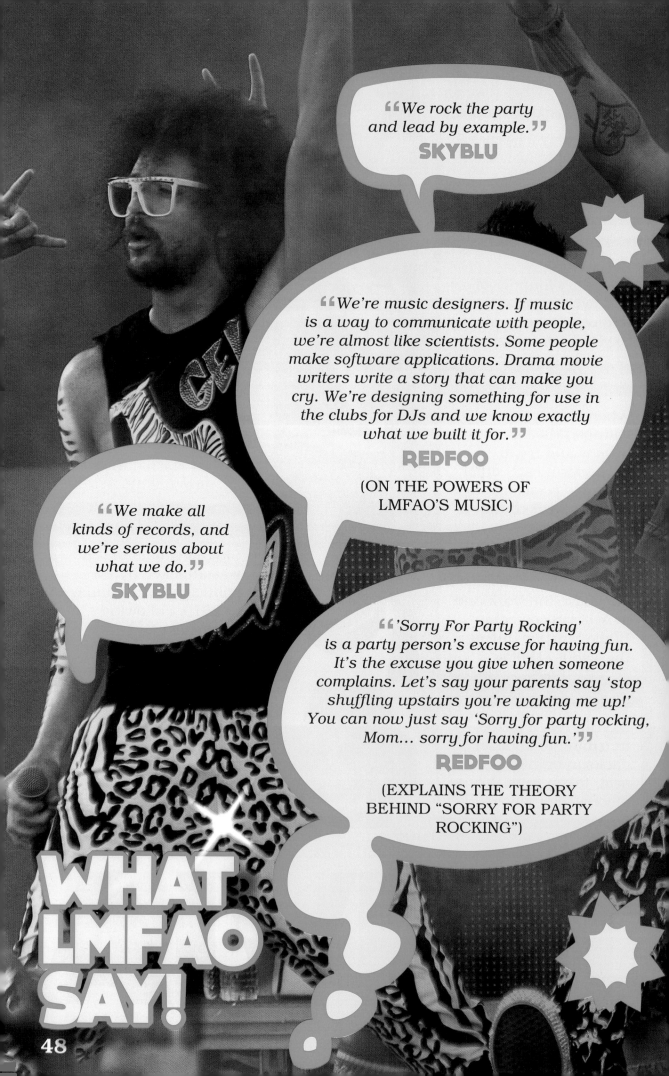

"We rock the party and lead by example." **SKYBLU**

"We're music designers. If music is a way to communicate with people, we're almost like scientists. Some people make software applications. Drama movie writers write a story that can make you cry. We're designing something for use in the clubs for DJs and we know exactly what we built it for." **REDFOO**

(ON THE POWERS OF LMFAO'S MUSIC)

"We make all kinds of records, and we're serious about what we do." **SKYBLU**

"'Sorry For Party Rocking' is a party person's excuse for having fun. It's the excuse you give when someone complains. Let's say your parents say 'stop shuffling upstairs you're waking me up!' You can now just say 'Sorry for party rocking, Mom… sorry for having fun.'" **REDFOO**

(EXPLAINS THE THEORY BEHIND "SORRY FOR PARTY ROCKING")

WHAT LMFAO SAY!

"There are no rules in dance music. It doesn't matter if you're rich or poor…'party' is a whole genre that everyone was discounting, but that's all we want to do. Who wouldn't want to be at a great party with sexy people?"

REDFOO

(EXPLAINS THE WHOLE REASON LMFAO EXISTS)

"I'm a real DJ. But I'm also a rapper… I grew up listening to Tupac, Mos Def and Eminem."

SKYBLU'S MUSICAL ROOTS

"My work ethic is for someone who wants to be number one."

LMFAO

(LIKE TO WORK HARD AND PARTY HARDER, OF COURSE!)

"That was one of the slickest videos ever. We were very inspired by (Michael Jackson's) 'Thriller', and to have an opportunity to do something like that is amazing. No one knows this about us, but we are high level athletes, and we go hard whether it's basketball, tennis, skateboarding or dancing."

SKYBLU

(ON THE UNFORGETTABLE VIDEO FOR PARTY ROCK ANTHEM, AND THEIR ATHLETIC CAPABILITIES)

A *'And I Know It'*: LMFAO's biggest hit to date has sparked copycat videos from all walks of life and has been used in countless TV shows and adverts. No matter how many times we hear it though, we'll never tire of the crazy beat.

B *Berry Gordy*: legendary US producer, founder of Motown records. Redfoo's father and SkyBlu's grandfather.

C *Champagne Showers*: single taken from 'Sorry for Party Rocking' featuring English singer Natalia Kills.

D *DJ*: both boys have regular DJ slots in some of the hippest clubs in the US. They know how to get the party rocking.

E *'Everyday I'm Shufflin'*: need we say more?

F *Facebook*: More than 18.5 million followers can't be wrong...

G *GoonRock*: producer, songwriter and musician. Co-wrote 'Party Rock Anthem' and 'I'm Sexy and I Know It'.

H *Hot Dog*: ode to post club snack favoured by the boys.

I *DJ Inphinity*: DJ & Producer, helped kick off LMFAO's success with a bootleg featuring the boys, called 'Bass Kick in Miami'.

J *Lil Jon*: collaborated with the boys on their single 'Shots' and his single 'Outta Your Mind'.

K *Ke$ha*: LMFAO opened for Ke$ha on her 2011 US tour.

L *Los Angeles*: both boys grew up in the affluent Pacific Palisades, an LA neighbourhood.

A TO Z
OF LMFAO!

M *Madonna*: LMFAO performed with the Queen of Pop at half time of the 2012 Super Bowl.

N *Nephew*: SkyBlu is Redfoo's nephew.

O *Over the Top*: their style their attitude and their music - there are no half measures in LMFAO's world!

P *Party Rock*: first album, featured 'I'm in Miami'.

Q *Quest Crew*: LA hip hop dance crew - one of their members choreographed the videos for 'Party Rock Anthem' and 'I'm Sexy and I Know It'.

R *Redfoo*: real name Stefan Kendal Gordy.

S *SkyBlu*: real name Sklyer Austen Gordy.

T *Tupac Shakur*: the LA rapper was an inspiration to both the boys.

U *Uncle*: Redfoo is SkyBlu's uncle.

V *Venice Beach*: where the video for 'I'm Sexy and I Know It...' was shot.

W *will.i.am*: childhood friend of Redfoo.

X *X Rated*: sometimes the boys can be a little cheeky...

Y *Yes*: last single taken from the Party Rock album.

Z *Led Zeppelin*: 70's rockers, lovers of tight jeans and big hair – the boys are huge fans.

PARTY ROCKIN' TUNES

If you're planning a party, really the easiest thing to do would be to get the two LMFAO albums, stick them on shuffle, and get shuffling... but occasionally you might like to mix in a few other tracks along the way. Even Redfoo and SkyBlu themselves love other people's music, and drop some killer tunes at their regular DJ sets. Here's a pick of their, and our, favourite tunes to get the party rocking!

KINGS OF LEON: 'SEX ON FIRE'

Ok, it may not be an obvious high-energy dance track, but the boys play a mean mixed up version of this in their set, rocking the dance floor.

DEADMAU5

The boys have worked with the Canadian producer on a number of projects, and they know any of his tracks will bring the house down!

THE BLACK EYED PEAS

will.i.am is a childhood friend of Redfoo, and the two have worked closely together ever since. As well as working in the studio together, the LMFAO boys often like to drop in Black Eyed Peas tracks to their DJ sets.

THE BEETROOTS

Italian house and dance-punk project have worked with LMFAO on remixes, and can often be found rocking their party.

MICHAEL JACKSON

Both the boys are huge MJ fans (in fact Michael's brother Jermaine was married to Redfoo's sister), and the pair grew up very close to the Jackson family. Their favourite tracks by the legend are:

Redfoo: 'Thriller' (for the video), the whole 'Thriller' album and also 'Man in the Mirror'.

SkyBlu: 'Lady of my Life', 'Baby be Mine'.

we *love* you...
LMFAO

54

we love you...
LMFAO

SPOT THE DIFFERENCE

We think the LMFAO boys look great in their outrageous outfits and crazy hairstyles, but can you spot the 7 differences between these pictures?

2012 was a pretty busy year for Redfoo and SkyBlu, the LMFAO boys, with many highlights – playing at the Superbowl with Madonna, winning so many awards, and having top ten hits all over the world.

They rounded off the year with Party Rockin performances at V Festival, a whistle stop tour round Europe, including DJ sets in the party island of Ibiza, and in the autumn, played seven dates in Las Vegas, grabbing a bit of sun before the winter kicked in – there were even rumours that the boys would be playing an awesome set in Las Vegas to celebrate New Years' Eve.

And what are the plans for the boys in 2013? Well, they must surely be thinking about making the most of their successes, and getting some new material out in the New Year.

There's no doubting that LMFAO are a total party band, but that doesn't mean they're not serious about their business, and have a plan for their future.

The boys are well-known for their dedication to the art of songwriting, and not just writing any old song, but really crafting a hit that gets into people's heads so much that they can't stop singing it. And of course, they've been successful at this so far, but LMFAO are deliberately taking their time writing new material, to ensure that it matches the high standards they've set for themselves so far – there's no churning out below-par songs for these boys. So, while the fans might be screaming out for new songs, we can be assured that when they do arrive, LMFAO will be rocking the party once more!

2013 will also see a new tour for LMFAO, throughout the US, and there are even rumours they will be on the bill for the world-famous Coachella music festival, in California in the spring.

Whatever the boys get up to in 2013, we're positive it will bring a smile to our faces and a spring in our step – keep the party rocking!

THE FUTURE FOR LMFAO

Y	K	A	H	S	E	K	G	M	T	Y		T	
L	Q	L	K	C	O	R	N	O	O	G		O	
T	K	B	P	C	N	X	I	M	W	P		B	
P	A	R	T	Y	K	N	K	R	B	A		E	
Y	S	K	Y	B	L	U	C	F	M	L		L	
B	X	Y	W	Y	G	A	O	P	Z	I		F	
F	N	E	N	W	N	O	R	G	C	S		F	
D	X	Y	S	N	O	G	U	T	Z	A		U	
H	L	F	O	F	B	E	O	X	J	D		H	
Y	D	D	D	Y	T	J	V	R	L	E		S	
W	A	E	P	T	V	C	J	L	D	S		V	
M	R	R	A	J	Z	M	D	X	L	Y		R	

QUIZ ANSWERS

MIAMI BERY

SHOWERS

VENICE

SKYLER BLACKEYEDPEAS

QUEST

THESHUFFLE

PARTYROCKING

CREW STEFAN

WHERE'S SKYBLU?